PUPPIES ARE DIFFERENT

DOROTHY ANN

Copyright © 2025 by Dorothy Ann

Published by Queen Anne's Lace Publishing
ISBN 978-1-968575-03-8

All rights reserved.

Parts of this publication may be used and reproduced with permission. Use in schools or for personal use do not need permission. For permission requests contact dorothy.ann.qal@gmail.com.

The story, all names, characters, and incidents portrayed in this production are fictitious. No identification with actual persons (living or deceased), places, buildings, and products is intended or should be inferred.

Book Cover by Queen Anne's Lace Publishing

All images are free to use for commercial purposes, or designed by the publisher.

Hardcover edition, 2025

NOTES FOR HELPERS

Thank you so much for picking up this book!

We sincerely hope you enjoy reading *Puppies are Different*. This book primarily highlights the unique differences that make us all wonderful.

However, you can also use the book to discuss how disabilities may affect others, how people are alike and different, and why differences are fun.

Have children use their imaginations to name the puppies and talk about what relationships they might have with one another.

The font in this book is Arial because it helps dyslexic readers read more easily.

THIS BOOK BELONGS TO:

_____

Look at all these puppies.
They are all the same.
The world would be so boring if it were this way.

**Some puppies are big.
Some puppies are small.**

Some puppies are short.
Some puppies are tall.

Some puppies are round, which is super great!

Some puppies are thin, growing bigger every day.

Some puppies like chew toys, squeakers, or ropes—

but every puppy loves a good joke!

Some puppies like anything put on their plate.

For others, trying new foods is something they hate.

Some puppies have wheels, and people do too!

They have just as much fun as me and you!

Some puppies have spots, people have vitiligo.

This causes patches, some white as snow.

Have you met people or puppies like these at the playground or school?

Puppies are different, and that's so cool.

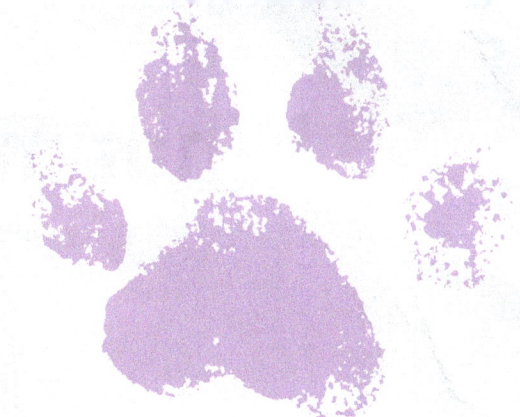

All puppies have feelings,
and hopes,
and big dreams.
Every single puppy is
wonderfully unique.

What makes you unique?

I AM UNIQUE:

ABOUT THE AUTHOR

Dorothy Ann lives in Ohio with her husband and two cats: Milo and Winston.

She loves reading, drawing, sewing, and hanging out with her family and friends.

She has two big dreams: to have an in-home library and to help friends like YOU fall in love with reading.

www.ingramcontent.com/pod-product-compliance
Lightning Source LLC
Chambersburg PA
CBHW060406010526
44107CB00005B/601